The Truck Driver's Wife

Holding Down The Home Front

SAUNDRA COVINGTON

Fulton Books, Inc.
Meadville, PA

Published by Fulton Books 2021

ISBN 978-1-63710-719-5 (paperback)
ISBN 978-1-63710-720-1 (digital)

Printed in the United States of America

This book is inspired by one of my favorite lines: "In dreams and in love, there are no impossibilities" (János Arany). This book is dedicated to my rock, my lovely husband, George. I thank God for bringing you in my life and blessing me with someone like you daily. Thank you for your love, support, encouragement, and for always keeping me smile. This book is a token of appreciation for you. We now have a written proof of all that we have been through and made it this far.

I love you always.

CONTENTS

ACKNOWLEDGMENTS

I would like to thank God for giving me the strength to go through with my plans; without my belief, nothing would be possible. To the women in my life—my mother, Lillian Lee, and grandmothers, for always having faith in me. I want to thank my sister and brother for keeping close to me even after all these years; the way we have kept our family strong even after mom and dad passed inspires me every day. Over these years, our love has only grown stronger. To the best nephews an auntie could ask for, they also gave me the idea to share my life journey and make me want to be a better human being every day. To be able to hold you in my arms is the best gift one could ever hope for.

CHAPTER 1

Meeting My Truck Driver

Fifteen years ago, I found the love of my life; when I met George, I had no idea he would be the light of my life, but here we are, fifteen years later. Meeting George was like finding the missing piece of my heart that I had been searching for.

A person who has worked every day since their sixteenth birthday, never realized what being a truck driver meant for them and their families. This is my journey; a story I keep close to my heart, a story I want everyone to hear.

This story dates back to November 12, the day I married my George, a truck driver, my soulmate and everything. My life had everything before I stumbled across someone like him, except him. However, it did not come easy nor was it as romantic as everyone makes it out to be.

"Love at first sight," I never believed in it, and I still do not. Every passing day that we spend more and more time together, I fall more in love, but there was never love at first sight.

Frankly, when I met George, I was not looking for anything, just maybe a free meal, because I thought to myself, *Who doesn't like a free meal? And with someone who's not too bad on the eyes.* So I agreed. He asked me if I would have dinner with him if he were ever in town, and I just agreed.

People often asked me if I thought and pondered how I chose this man, but if I am honest…he is the one who picked me. I always say, "You don't pick your truck driver, the truck driver picks you," which is exactly what happened. He picked me, and suddenly I felt at home.

On a Saturday evening, in Ontario, California, I was having dinner with my cousin, and this bald tall brown-eyed person walked toward me. He was not shy, nor was he embarrassed about asking me out immediately. I thought to myself *What the hell? It is a free meal after all*, so I took his number and thought if he ever passed through town again, we would get together.

It is an obvious thing: when you think of a life partner, you do not picture someone who is out of town five days out of seven, but here I was, agreeing to take my chances for a free meal and good company.

We immediately talked, and suddenly, I felt like I was being pushed closer to him. I still feel like God was the one stringing things along; everything was falling into place.

I spent the next few days thinking about our conversations together when we grabbed dinner. Soon after, he asked me if I would be able to drive down to Arizona for a few hours to spend the weekend. I kept thinking to myself, *No, what are you doing? Why would you drive four hours to go to a strange city with a man you barely know?* But before I could even think of a response, I heard my voice agreeing to go see him. I thought a lot about why I had done that but left it up to fate and the gut feeling I had about this wonderful truck driver, my truck driver.

I called my parents to let them know about my weekend plans; my dad told me to have fun, but my mom was skeptical and asked why I had decided to go; again, I had no response. So I went. During the journey, I had called him a few times, but his phone was not reachable; I panicked slightly but decided to keep driving. Soon after, I got a call from him, apologizing and asking if I was still coming. To my surprise, before even thinking about my response, I heard my voice saying, "Yes, I'm still coming." That is how I spent one of the most thrilling weekends of my life getting to know this wonderful man.

However, this story is not just about the fairytale that we both shared the first few months of our relationship; it includes the most heartbreaking incidents that happened to the both of us; it kept us together. Our relationship started as a lottery box. I got lucky, but that is not what kept it going. George and I have been together for fifteen years; we have gone through a bankruptcy phase, heartache, distance, and the unbearable loss of losing a child. Yet, we stand in front of everyone stronger than ever.

Moving on, our life was a fairytale; we had discussed everything. Family, careers, and even the weight of being away from him was not as bad as I thought it would be, because at the end of the day, he was always going to come home to me, and I wanted to be that home to him. I always craved the feeling of belonging to someone, and with him, I felt like I belonged.

Being a truck driver's partner was never going to be easy; I knew this when I got closer to him, but there was something about him that drew me closer to him. Maybe it was the way he always made me feel at home; there was never a shred of doubt. I knew he was going to come to me, and he did. Every time he would leave to be on the road, he took a piece of me with him; and every time he came back, the piece just fit in again. You know that feeling that you were incomplete, there was always a piece missing from you; and then one day, you meet someone and all the pieces come together, and that's not even half the intensity with which I love him.

An all-consuming, overwhelming love. Chaotic, but calm. Loud but soft, a tornado of feelings but never drowning in love. That is what I feel for him, and he for me.

Fast forward, everyone told me this was the honeymoon period, and that it would end just as intensely as it began. Neither of us believed these people because people always like to see the worst-case scenarios, but truth be told, I always knew it would be him and me at the end of the road.

He is the light at the end of the tunnel, I thought to myself on a Sunday morning. I pinched myself, bringing me back to my daily life. *Why was I thinking about this man at 10:00 a.m. on a Sunday morning? Is this what love really felt like?* I pondered.

My phone dinged; it was a text from him. He has asked me to watch a movie with him. Thinking back, the movie was an action movie; the only kind he liked to watch. I responded immediately, not letting him know that I was thinking about him constantly.

It was mid-September; I was getting ready for the movies. I had no idea what I was going to be walking into when I said yes to the movie. I got dressed; he picked me up quarter to six. We got to the movies early. He looked happy. His brown eyes lightened every time he looked at me, and I loved that. I loved his eyes on me. On that day, it felt like he was waiting to tell me something. Nevertheless, I shrugged the feelings off and told myself it was because of the movies.

We sat down; the movie was about to start in a few minutes. He looked as happy as I had ever seen him. I thought to myself, I was in love. I really was in love. The movie started; the whole time, he watched the movie excitedly while I watched him.

Soon after the movie was over, we went back to the apartment and sat cozily on the sofa, when he got down on one knee and proposed to me. For a split second, I thought back to the fact that I met this man four months ago and how my life has changed by his presence, but I also thought about how my life was going to change further. Being a truck driver's wife, it was not going to be easy. How could it be easy? Spending hours with your husband before he leaves to be on the road again, we would be living entirely different lives.

I heard myself say, "Yes, I agree." Suddenly, all the doubts and questions in my mind disappeared. It was the happiest day of our lives. We finally belonged, and we belonged together. Even after agreeing, I felt like we needed some time to get to know each other. I felt like he needed to get to know my family, and I his.

We spent a year after our engagement getting to know each other's families, little quirks of daily life, and the twelve months served as nothing but an immense overload of love and respect for each other. The year went by in a flash; I got my church involved so I would be sure of him and our future together.

Our life began; we went through many phases together; our life slowly unraveled in front of our eyes. We lost a child. The pain was unbearable, but we got through it together. We felt the pain of losing a child and all our money; we built our life together from scratch.

CHAPTER 2

Marriage

Marriage: the meeting of two souls, compromise, love, friendship, and showing up. Every day that I spend with George, I believe in it more—the definition of marriage is for me. Marriage, to me, was never a fairytale. This minute I said I do, I was his and he was mine. However, I knew it was not going to be easy.

When we started dating, the plan was always to go six months without proposing or talking about marriage, but that did not work. The plan went to hell the minute he proposed in four months of our relationship. We drove immediately to my parent's house, and my whole family was surprised. Later, I sat down with mom; she talked about what to expect as a truck driver's wife.

We spent the weekend in Vegas and had a wonderful time talking about our wedding and marriage, the date, where we will be living, and everything that came with the decision to get married. I had so many questions for him, his family, does he get angry; he was always so calm. We spent hours talking, talking about each other's lives, then we picked the date.

In the relationship, I had many cultural shocks and one religious struggle. Initially, when George decided to move in with me before our marriage, I asked my aunt about how it would be for me religiously. Her answer shocked me because she was calm and accepting of it. She reassured me about him living with me. I had never lived with a man before; that was just new to me, but it was a wonderful experience.

We even did a marriage class with my pastor at the church; even after he was on the road, he would take the classes with me on the phone. The marriage class helped me in many ways; we found a lot about our personalities in that class. The initial shock of a wedding proposal, people, things we do not want to talk about, the heavy stuff, but we did. We had arguments, disagreements, even long debates; it made me see who he was and for him to see who I was.

Diving into the wedding day itself, a girl's dream, a wedding dress, her wedding dress is what everyone wants to hear about. I got the wedding dress in March, even though the wedding was not until November. I wanted to start looking; I wanted just to check my options. However, I would not say I fell in love with George at first sight, but when I saw that beautiful bridal dress from David's, I fell in love. I bought it, and it spent six months in my mom's room.

The wedding event was small, cozy, and wonderful. We had the closest members of our families with us; it was held at my church. I never wanted something extravagant; I wanted something simple and cute. Even my bridesmaids did not include extra people. However, when I had my bachelorette party, everyone was there. We partied for hours in San Diego. At the wedding, my brother walked me down the aisle; it was one of the best moments of my life, but I started crying the minute before I had to walk down the aisle. Halfway down the aisle, I stopped walking, and my brother looked at me, confused, and asked, "Do you want to go back? We can go back," and I said I just needed a moment to collect myself. Next thing I know, I hear George's mom yelling at George, "Go get her, George," and he smiled at me. I thought to myself, I was not unsure of this man. I was just so overwhelmed with all the tasks and all the chores. Ta-da, we were done.

Just like that, we were now husband and wife. We had the reception Downtown Long Beach with great views; however, like every wedding, we had a little flaw. George lost his extra pair of shoes; he wanted to change shoes when we got to the wedding reception. Alas, we never found the shoes. The shoes caused him not to be able to dance a lot, but we had fun. We danced a lot, which was the most beautiful day of my life.

The next morning, I woke up thinking, *I don't feel different*, it just felt normal. We felt like we fit; I woke up happy in the morning; we had breakfast and took his uncle to the airport. The next day, while opening gifts, we even ate the cake topper. There were not many conventional traditions with us. I always heard that you are supposed to save the cake topper for your first anniversary. Still, George and I thought we are not conventional, so we enjoyed it for dessert.

We were back in our work life; he went back on the road, and I went back to my work. Now, I had decisions to make, my maiden name, my job. I spent hours thinking if I wanted to change my name. I thought to myself about how men never have to think about these things. I did not concern him with my thoughts; he left it to me. He was back on the road now, and I could not worry him about this while he was on the road. He needs to be focused when he drives. This is what we felt, the things we felt, and this is how our story unraveled after the wedding.

Now began the marriage part. Growing up, I always had this dream, a series of fairytale events were planned in my head that always made it seem like once I was married, I would have a perfect life. My husband would go to events with me; I would never be alone anymore. This is what marriage meant to me, but I did not know what God had planned for me.

The reality was that I married a truck driver; he was on the road. If he were not on the road, he was not making money, so he had to drive. In the beginning, it upset me to no ends; I felt like my childhood dream was fading from me. I felt like I was doing it all alone; every event I would go to, people would ask about George. I would answer he is working. There were no set scheduled in this industry, and he was working.

What made it special, though, was the fact that every time he was home, he made sure he would come with me to events, even though he was tired and not interested. This is what marriage is to me.

The effort that George put after hours and hours of being on the road, coming home to me, and then going to events just to be with me. Granted that he was falling asleep at every one of those events, but the fact that he was showing up, every time, that is what marriage is. I wanted to show him off; I wanted to show my man off after thirty-five years. I deserved that.

Sometimes I would slightly hit him when he would fall asleep at certain events, not realizing that he was doing his best. We spent hours later talking about it, and he told me when he gets home, he needs rest before getting out. It took me a long time to adjust to it, his schedule. It took about a year for me to understand and adjust to his schedules and then prioritize what was important. This made me feel like we were adults, and we were not just two kids in a relationship.

Often, it was fleeting moments. He would come home to say hi, quick shower, grab a plate, and then go. It was no longer just about spending the most time at events. The minute we got married, I transformed into a wife, a best friend, a secretary, and still holding down my full-time career because George was not around much. But that is what it was? Sometimes I wondered, *Was I doing too much? Was it all just him, him, and him?*

The word "compromise" showed up many times; I hated it. The word echoed in my brain for hours at one point, but I realized it came with the marriage. Being a truck driver's wife, I knew what I was getting into. It took us some time, but we found a balance; it was no longer just me making all the efforts anymore.

At home, we found a balance. He takes care of the outside, and I take care of the inside. He makes breakfast, and I make dinner. It never went just one person doing everything, while the other relied on them.

"The honeymoon phase," I heard about this phase so much. Growing up, everyone around me talked about this magical period that couples would have and then hit a rut. I expected that to happen, but George and I, we had an unconventional marriage. After our wedding, he went on the road. We did not get a honeymoon period; we went straight into the in and out of the marriage itself. Therefore, it was only fair that I say we lived the honeymoon period, and we are still living it. Every hardship that we had to face, every time we showed up for each other, that is what honeymoon was for me.

Amid all the angst, the frustration of not seeing each other, money problems, and even losing a child, we were there. We showed up even after I gave him a way out to leave after my miscarriage, but he stayed. This is what dedication felt like, the willingness to make it work through thick and thin—that is what the honeymoon phase should mean and not just meaningless grand gestures.

Even after years of our marriage, I still feel like I will never stop fully knowing him. In the middle of conversations, we realize how much people change and alter themselves together, so we grow together and deal with all the changes together.

On our tenth wedding anniversary, he brought up something I told him ten years ago. We made a pact when we were dating that there would be no exes involved. I told him, "I don't want that in ten years. Someone would be coming up to the door and saying, 'Hi, Daddy,'" so he brought it up after ten years, and we laughed it off. This little gimmick meant so much to me; he remembered something so small just to be able to laugh it off after ten years. That is when I realized that we made it. For ten years, with or without our marriage, we go for date nights. We celebrate us. We talked, and we laughed about little things over our little cake. These were the kind of traditions we keep, the nonconventional ones and the ones that make you feel at peace.

The first time that we argued, it was after we got married. I realized something. I thought to myself, *There is no escape. He will not leave, and I cannot leave too. This person is not going home.* I felt like that was the light for me. Regardless of the arguments and disagreements, we had to stick together, and that is a feeling that was not fleeting; it stayed. However, I also feel like when he goes on the road, I get a little time to breathe, and that took some time to adjust to.

With all the hardships that come with being a truck driver's wife, the good parts are just as fascinating. Every time that he comes home to me, it feels just as amazing as it did the first time. Every time he comes home, we have a home-cooked meal, and we talk about our lives; and each time, it is just as amazing as the first.

This is what marriage is for us; each couple goes through different things, but I will always feel like we made our own marriage rules, and that is when even on our tenth anniversary, we were just as giddy as we were on that first date.

CHAPTER 3

The Child...Or Not

Showing up, day after day, and being there was what makes a marriage successful. However, the road to a successful marriage is never easy; sometimes, it even breaks your heart.

George and I loved kids; we had always talked about them and always wanted to have one or two of our own. A tiny little me running around our patio with yellow onesie, or a sweet little George with a head full of hair. We wanted that, and I wanted to give that to my husband.

When we first met, George and I moved significantly faster than normal couples; we were never conventional. We discussed things, talked about having a small family, which obviously included the decision of wanting children at one point in our lives. The discussion was so right on, that right before we got married, I got off the pill and we began trying.

When George and I got married, we were already in our midthirties, and when you are in your thirties, you have had plenty of time to think about the kind of family you want. Both of us already knew we both wanted at least two or three kids, a baby girl first. When our wedding was getting closer, I went to see my physician and got off the pill. This was how ready I was, and he was. We wanted to have a family right away.

A few days before Thanksgiving, I went to the doctor because I was feeling a bit off and took some tests. When I was driving home, I got a call from the doctor. She told me I was pregnant; I was beyond ecstatic. I pulled over, found the courage to form sentences to say, "Thanks you, God." She congratulated us. Now began the planning of how to tell George. You know, you see all these videos and movies clips about how to break the news to your man. All of them started repeatedly replaying in my head; I had to shrug them off immediately. My husband was an over-the-road driver, and it could be weeks before he came home.

I got home, sat down to collect my thoughts, and then called George. I told him I was pregnant, and he went completely silent. My heart dropped. *Was this not what he wanted?* I thought to myself. Then I heard a loud "YES, BABY!" however, which interrupted my thought that he said out lout expressing his excitement. I sighed in relief. He told me he could not wait to see me and how excited he was to come home.

Normally, you would think a thirty-six-year-old woman getting pregnant for the first time would have some emotions and some built-up anticipation to get rid of, but I did not. Everything went back to normal immediately. I told my parents and family; everyone was beyond excited.

My mom had always hoped for an adorable granddaughter because boys surrounded my family. While at home, I made lists about what I would need, calculated my days off that I would need after the baby comes, thinking about how much time George would like off, and what we would need to save; if the wheels are not rolling, no money comes in.

A few days later, he comes home. I had never seen him so happy; there was a different glow in his eyes. A spark I had not seen before. I loved that I gave that to him. We spent a happy Christmas together and had an amazing time at New Year's dinner discussing baby names.

The day after New Year, I felt sick. I thought to myself, *My baby does not like Chinese.* I chuckled and thought nothing of it. George was going back to work; he kissed the baby and me and left.

Now, two days had passed, and I was still feeling a bit sick. I decided to go to the doctor. However, I was told it was my body adjusting because it was my first pregnancy. I was still skeptical but came home.

The next few hours, I spent talking to my baby, but somewhere around 11:00 p.m., I started feeling sick again. I called the nurse and asked her about it. She advised me to take something with me to the bathroom in case something comes out. The minute I heard those words, I panicked. I had never been pregnant before, and this made me uncomfortable just thinking about it.

After the call, I called George to let him know that I was going to call my mother to take me to the hospital, which she did. It was midnight by the time we started tests; the doctors did two ultrasounds and found out that the fertilized egg was implanted in my tube and was about to rupture.

The second I found out, my mind went into panic mode.

They suggested immediate surgery to get it removed, I refused. I did not want to go in without my husband. This was major; he should be here with me, I thought to myself. However, around 2:00 a.m., I had to be taken into surgery; my mother reassured me that they would keep trying to reach him. However, George was delivering a load in the Everglades and would be out of signals until the next morning when he was finished. The next morning, when I woke up, mom said that they spoke with him and would find a truck stop and fly out as soon as possible.

When George got there, we sat and I cried. I apologized to him for losing our child. Even though the doctor said it was not anything I did, my heart still broke. At that time, the doctors had told us that we would still be able to conceive later; we had a miscarriage. However, misery did not end here.

The morning after the surgery, the doctor told me that I have had a fever, which could potentially be an infection, which is why I could not be discharged from the hospital. The doctor had also informed us of the possibility of a hysterectomy in my case if the infection does not go away.

The thought of a hysterectomy made me anxious; at this point, both George and I were panicking a little. The next morning, I got some tests done, and then eventually, I found out that the infection was still there, and I needed the hysterectomy.

We had no other options; getting the hysterectomy was the only way to treat the infection. However, getting the hysterectomy meant I would never be about to give birth.

The realization hit harder than we expected; not only did we lose our child but were now told I would never be able to give birth. I looked over at George; he remained calm and asked the doctor when he would be able to make love to me, and we all laughed.

I was now preparing for the surgery, had to drink lots of bad fluid for it. George and I got a chance to talk; I apologized to him and gave him a way out of the marriage. I knew how much he wanted kids, and I would never be able to give him that. He responded calmly, "I did not marry you for your tube or your eggs. I married you because I love you." The minute I heard those words come from his mouth, I felt calm. I was no longer worrying.

After the surgery, my mom and sister took me home. George had to get back to work to get his truck that he had left at the truck stop. He would call every two hours from the road to check up on me. I was not falling apart, but some part of me was incredibly sad.

The aftereffects were worse. I would be driving to work and see women with their children and find myself wondering. Oftentimes, I would question God about why it had to be me. I would think about the fact that I did everything I could. I waited for the right man. I never had any pregnancy scares; I did everything right. I would find myself breaking down in the shower, thinking about what could have been, thinking about our little family, our plans.

However, each one of these feelings was fleeting because I was beyond grateful for what God had blessed me with.

The journey to getting better was long and bitter; it took me two years before I could go to another baby shower and come to terms with what had happened.

George and I had planned to move out of state, but we were waiting to have kids. Now that has changed. We could move our plan up and adopt when we relocate. We thought of adopting a girl; we started taking classes, but again, George had to be on the road, so we had to skip most of it.

The lack of time and our mismatching schedules made us reconsider our decision of bringing a child into our chaotic lifestyle; we decided to put it off.

When I was laid off, I got a job, working in a call center. We started the classes again. However, it felt like destiny had a different plan for us.

Not a lot of days after our classes, we had a family meeting and discussed the unavailability because of the nature of our jobs and how it would affect a child, him on the road, and now me working third shift in a call center. how that would affect a child. We decided against it. It was not fair on the child. It felt like we were once again losing our dream, but this time, it was forever.

Losing our child felt like a part of me had died with him/her, but eventually, we had to get back on track. The best part was that we had each other.

You read stories about how in times of adversity, couples fall apart. At the back of my mind, I always wondered if that would ever happen. It never did. Every day, George showed me why I chose him; and every day, we grew closer to each other.

It was now time to get back to our life. We started piecing our life together bit by bit; I started volunteering at the Foster Care Review Board; my little way to help the kiddos. Arizona was a little lonely when he was at work, so I began making friends, getting involved in the community, and getting back to existence, which I loved.

Amid all this pain and misery, we kept our light moments. We kept our little surprises along with us. George would surprise me by coming home early from the road with plush toys; every time he came home earlier than usual, I would get butterflies.

While the tubal pregnancy taught me many things, the biggest lesson it taught me was the fact that nothing else matters when your significant other is supportive, which is why we kept our romantic moments even after having been through something so traumatic. Such as when I would pick him up at the yard, I would flash him, luckily no one was there to enjoy it other than him. Oftentimes, I would also tape my lingerie to the garage door so when he pulled up, he'll see that. It kept the spark of romance in our relationship alive.

At the end of the day, we went through the biggest loss we could possibly imagine and got through it. Together.

CHAPTER 4

Filing for Bankruptcy

Here begin the money problems. Getting into a marriage, you expect things to be easier financially. When George and I met, we were already in our midthirties, working and thinking about starting a family. Even though the latter did not work out, we still had hopes about our financial situation to go even higher than before. However, the universe had other plans for us.

After our miscarriage, George and I had started a trucking business because we wanted to invest in ourselves and hoped to be fluttering as soon as the profits rolled in. Needless to say, the plan did not go as we hoped.

We started the trucking business with lots of hopes and dreams, but we forgot the first rule of business: having a capital investment or savings to begin with, so when the profits were coming, they all went to the fueling and the upkeep of the trucks. Things started happening, mechanical difficulties, and any money that was made was put into the business and home.

During this time, with my check and little coming from business, that was barely enough to keep us afloat. The expenses kept rolling in. When the mechanical expenses started piling up, we felt we were drowning. Before starting the business, we had no idea it would come crashing down on us before even taking off properly.

The more time that was passing, we were going under constant stress because of the lack of built-up capital. Any money that we were making off the business was being put right back into the business. A couple months had passed now, we were still hoping for a miracle.

As the time went by, we needed to pay taxes, and money was not flowing in as we hoped. This put us in a hurdle. I decided to not pay money to IRS because the choice was between that money being put to keeping our house. At this point, we were down to twenty dollars groceries per week.

When we were starting the business, we had hoped for profits showing after two months in. Everyone has goals and wants to be their own boss, which is what we wanted too.

However, the more time that was passing, our dreams felt like they were fading. We had a dream and kept going.

Eight months down the line, he called a family meeting. This is one of the most important things in our marriage. A meeting, an official meeting between the two of us, where we can voice our concerns and then make an informed decision. We decided that we would sell the truck, and George would go back on road working for a company.

I agreed with what he was saying. He made a quick decision to get us out of this before we drowned. I followed his lead. I trusted him when we decided to start the business, and now that he had decided to pull us out, I trusted him with this too.

We lasted about eight months in the business, and then we talked and discussed that it was not working. We were stuck in a rut with our business, and it was not working the way we thought.

However, while we ended the business and George went back to work for a company, things were not as simple as just ending the business; the domino effect had already started because of the loans that we took out to invest in the business. Since money was slowly coming in, our bills were barely being paid.

While things were still not stable, we were happier. George looked happier now; he had no stress. Somehow, amid all this chaos, his smiling face calmed all the storms we had coming our way.

Eventually, we talked about credit-line servicing and did our best with what we could. However, it seemed that filing bankruptcy was our only option left.

This decision was not easy; after I was laid off, bankruptcy was an option. One day, when I went to work on Monday, my manager called others and me in the conference room and informed us of budget cuts and said sorry we were being laid off. I have never been laid off before; I have always been a working woman ever since I was sixteen. This came as a complete shock. I felt like the floor had left from under my feet and did not know what to do.

I drove back home, silently went up to George to tell him that I had been laid off; his initial response was disbelief; he thought I was joking.

We talked that night and decided to file for bankruptcy. Our credit card payments and loans were getting harder to manage every day. We filed for bankruptcy; this was when a heavyweight was lifted off our shoulders. After months, I finally felt like I could breathe. We finally got a clean slate, one where we can work forward from. I had to start looking for a job and slowly be okay with not working for the time being.

The filing for bankruptcy was thankfully made easier for us. Because of my previous company's severance package, we were able to get a bankruptcy attorney.

The whole eight to ten months of the business starting, ending, and then us filing for bankruptcy had been a rollercoaster.

I was not even sure how I felt about all of this; between all of this, I did not have the time to sit down and process any of it. I just kept going forward, working with what we had, and trying to hold down the home. George was stressed; he was constantly worried about me from the road, which led him to decide on coming back home and taking a different job to be home more often.

Once again, through thick and thin. Through sickness and health, and now, through rich and poor. We had stuck together; we were drowning, but together. This is why we made it; we stayed afloat until we found the anchor that pulled us back to the shore.

CHAPTER 5

Drowning Together

"Together forever" seems such a long way to go when you vow to love each other on your wedding day, but when you get married to the love of your life, life passes you by in seconds. George and I had the most nonconventional relationship, and now a nonconventional marriage.

We vowed to help each other through sickness and any troubles, to never let the other person go through anything alone. I never thought these things would come up in our lives, but they did. Filing for bankruptcy, our business failing, losing a child, having financial constraints, and switching jobs were not easy on either of us.

Before any of our moves, we were dealing with a credit card servicing, which at the time felt like a good idea, but in hindsight, it was now the best decision to leave that. It was only harming our finances even worse than before.

Even during all chaos that we were dealing with, at the time of us shutting down our business, we took mini trips; this was possible because George and I made plans months every year before and made monthly payments. While many people would have postponed their trips, we did not. We went, which helped us gain our composure to deal with the life we had back home. These little trips relaxed us and helped keep us focus on our goals and still enjoy each other.

Back home, when we filed bankruptcy and got a window to breathe and let it unwind, we felt like we were finally relieved. However, what awaited us was worse. I was laid off. However, being laid off was the worst thing that could have happened to us at the moment.

I grew up in a female career-oriented family; my mom, grandmother, and sister were always keen on long-term careers and building savings, which was passed down to me. Ever since I turned sixteen, I had constantly been working, bought my first home at twenty-nine years old. This is who I was; this is how I identified myself. Someone who works hard, and now for the first time since I was sixteen, I was a forty-year-old woman who was unemployed.

The minute I was told that I would no longer be working for Arizona State, I felt like I was being choked and the air was being sucked out of the room that I was in, but when I looked around, everything was normal. I drove back home worrying and thinking about what would happen; George was home. He had taken a security job and left his trucking job to be home, which also meant less money. I got home and spoke to George, and he reassured me everything would be okay.

I got home and spoke to George; everything he said calmed me down. I felt more secure. However, the security job was not working out for him; he was not happy doing it. We had a family meeting right after; we sat down to discuss what the next move would be. While I felt extremely upset that he would have to leave again, I knew he needed to go in order to be happy and to keep his family afloat. Therefore, we both agreed that he would go back on the road.

Once again, we were going to be apart. However, this time, I put forward demands about him going on the road. I told him to only do eleven western states this time around, and he would not be gone any longer than seven to eight days at once. To which, he agreed.

Now, I began the job hunt. This was a painful process, never having been through this. I was out of practice, all day every day, I was on my laptop. I was looking for new opportunities to join. I spent hours moping around the house, while George worried about me on the road.

Every day he would call to ask about the update, and I would be looking through thousands of job openings only to spend the next few days waiting for an interview call. I felt useless, a feeling I had never felt before.

A couple months before this, I was swamped with work, keeping the house running. Things had changed, and I was having difficulty adjusting to what I was going to do next.

George, however, had full faith in me. Even on days when I was losing faith in myself, he stuck through and kept me motivated. Even when he was on the road, he never missed our regular phone calls.

Even during my worst days, I felt calm when we talked. After ten years of our marriage, I knew I could confine in my husband the way I did the first time I met him. During the six months that I had no job, I continued to grow closer to him. I was not alone.

It was a random Tuesday evening when my phone rang. I answered immediately, thinking it might be a job interview.

"Hey," I heard George's heavy but soulful voice on the other end of the line; I asked him how he was and what was up. He told me to pack my bags and get dressed. "You are coming with me."

At first, I was a bit taken aback, thinking it was a joke. George and I have always had little pranks that we do when he is away on a trip. He surprises me by being home early, so I thought this might be one of those times.

It was not though he was serious. I questioned him about the interview calls, about how we would have the internet on the road. He calmly explained that we would manage; we just needed to get out, have a trip just the two of us.

After much hesitation, I agreed. He was right; we made stops at hotels, restaurants, and shops where we got the internet for me to send out more applications, along with checking to see if I had gotten any replies. We waited for an interview call, but it never came.

The trip, however, was amazing. I had never been on the road with him like this. He was in his element, but he felt at peace, and so did I.

We spent the entire trip talking, discussing, enjoying, and having the most fun we had in a long time. It helped me declutter my brain and helped George not be constantly worried about me moping around the house.

Through it all, we stuck together and stayed stronger than ever. The motivation, the love, is what kept us together. We were drowning, but together, and that is what pulled us out of the ocean.

CHAPTER 6

Cutting Down

Being a truck driver's wife was not going to be easy, I knew that. I entered this marriage prepared for that. However, I did not know it was going to be this hard. I had always heard that it was a different lifestyle. Being away from your husband for weeks, it was never going to be an easy path, but we took it. For years, we made it work for us and built our future together.

We spent many wonderful years before we decided that it was time for us to cut down, not that this decision was a personal choice, but something we knew we needed to do. After filing for bankruptcy, we realized we had hit a rough patch, and it was time to start prioritizing things.

During the time when George and I started our own business, we made some lousy business decisions that involved low capital investment and made us lose a lot of money. Now, when we had left the business and were starting fresh, there were many things to do. So George and I filed for bankruptcy because I was laid off and he had to find a new trucking company to work with.

Eventually, after six months of struggling here and there, I landed a job. However, the pay for this job was not what I was making six months ago. In theory, this was not a bad opportunity, and I needed the job, so I took it. Even after taking the job, I was quite disheartened for not being able to make as much as I was making before; the feeling was starting to settle in.

I love my job. I still do. It was one of the best decisions to take it when I did, but when you have worked all your life, getting a pay downgrade feels like a stab in your back. I felt like I was going backward; my goals were always set, and I was there, but now suddenly, everything was going one step back. This is how I felt but seeing George work so hard for us only made me want to work things out and keep going. Which is exactly what I did.

Slowly, things were getting steady again. However, because of the bankruptcy and the cut in our combined salaries now, we sat down to talk about how we were going to regroup and built our life back together.

This is what I love about us; the fact that even during times where we could have just lived paycheck to paycheck, our family meetings saved us. We decided together and acted on it. Four years down the line, it had paid off.

During a family meeting we had, George and I discussed leaving the house we were currently in. It was a four-bedroom home, 1800 square meters, that we did not really need all that space. We realized that we were up above our means and were now rebuilding our life, which meant putting our dream house on hold for a while.

We did a short sale on the house we were living in and, instead, decided to rent a house. This was a major life-changing event, and we did it to cut down on our expenses.

Living in a different house for three years, we slowly realized that it was not getting us to the point of savings that we had thought of. This did not mean that it was not less expensive; it just was not what we were hoping for.

We had another family meeting, after three years of living in a rented house, we talked and discussed the possible things we could be doing to help boost our expenses. The talk led to something I personally thought I would never agree to, but I did. We decided to rent an apartment instead of a house.

The last time I had lived in an apartment was back in my twenties; this came as a huge shock to the way I had been living for so many years. We downsized completely, which meant no luxury items, including the internet and no direct television. Overall, we cut down on four-hundred-dollar worth of expenses. Talking about it now, it feels absurd. We both had a vision, and we knew what we had to do to get there. Cutting down on all these expenses really helped boost our savings, which meant the more we cut down, the quicker we would be able to move to our dream house.

The dream house was our end goal, but trying to get there felt like a fight every day. Our apartment was small but felt smaller after years of having a lot of empty space around. Having one parking spot, always having to adjust times to be able to get a parking spot. We were also barely using any of our stuff; we got small stuff from Amazon and got rid of most of our stuff.

It was home, only when we were there. That was also one of the biggest factors. George and I barely spent any time there. This was during the time my mom had been diagnosed with cancer; my days off were spent in California. I had work, and he was on the road. The whole year we lived there we just came home to either sleep or be together, and when we were together, every place felt like home.

Living in an apartment only felt like a huge step back to me because of how I had been brought up. I had an apartment in my early twenties when I started my life, and now having to move back to an apartment and accepting a new career, making less money, felt like going backward. A small apartment, small space all felt too overwhelming to me. It felt like we were stuck in a rut.

Even amid all this downsizing and fitting into a new lifestyle, we felt like we had everything together. Even when we were squeezing in with our temporary but new life, everything fell into place, knowing we were in this together. On some days, we would sit and think about everything we had gone through and everything we still had to go through; it felt surreal.

This whole journey of downsizing taught me a lot of things, but the most important thing it taught me was that I had taken for granted what my life was. Being a trucker's wife was not an easy job, nor was it made for everyone. People give up, or feel lost, but the love George and I had made everything worth it.

The downsizing process took us four to five years to finally get back to our feet. There were many dark fleeting moments that often feel stupid now, but they were valid then. I often found myself wondering about what could have been. I had given up my beautiful house in California and moved to an unknown state with the love of my life. Even during those low moments, I never caught myself putting blame on George, or our relationship. It was never about what I had done, but what we had built together, and I would not trade that for a million townhouses.

With the downsizing, we were saving a lot, but even during this time, George had gone through three different companies because of the company's closing, or the load stopping. Sometimes, it felt like we were not making progress; the weeks where George was looking for another company to work for, we would have to use our savings to be able to get by.

Many people who go through financial troubles report that the love disappears when it comes down to monetary things disappearing from their lives. In my relationship with George, I saw the opposite. We had always been comfortable sharing our space without having to spend money on things. Even during the trouble we were having, we kept our little date nights and our trips constant. This is something I will always stand by; keeping the spark alive is what kept us sane throughout these years.

The only major discussion or argument per say that came up during these years was when we decided that I should get a car. George was initially against the idea because it felt like it was an added expense. At the time, we had only one car, the SUV that we bought when we got married, but the gas mileage on an SUV was astronomical.

Going to work alone was costing me hundred dollars on fuel every week, which seemed like a stupid added expense. We had many family discussions about this decision because it felt like a big step, but it was one that needed to be taken. The gas mileage was just a push that led to buying a car, because many times, having one car felt like it was paralyzing to the other person, being dependent on the other for errands.

Our credit was building slowly and steadily; we were getting back to where we wanted to be. The apartment really helped us reach our goal even faster than we had imagined. Our plan was to rent the apartment for two years and then get our own house; however, we only stayed in the apartment for a year and then moved out.

We moved out. It was time to live our dream. After spending four years going back and forth on our expenses, we finally could afford a new house. Our dream house concept had changed over the years. It was not big; it was just enough for the two of us. We barely have overnight guests, so we kept our house's open-floor plan; the kitchen opens into the dining room, a den for George, and one guest bedroom apart from ours.

We had gotten rid of most our stuff from the previous house. We sold things online and given things away to other people. So even our stuff was not hoarded.

After four years of struggles, we moved to a new life. Even after all the changes we went through, the one thing that remained constant was our love.

CHAPTER 7

Looking for an Adventure

Growing up, the meaning of adventure was just going on long trips and planned outings. Marrying George, my perception of everything changed, most of all, of what I thought life actually was.

Spending days away from your husband puts many things in perspective. This included the way we thought of our time together. Each time we would go on our cruise or on a little vacation getaway, it would feel just as special as it did the first time we went away together. Each time George came back home from work, it felt like he was coming home for the first time. This is what it meant to me. Our entire life was now an adventure that I got to share with the love of my life.

My family consists of my two siblings, our parents and me. Both my siblings are younger than I am. I have four handsome nephews, who are a huge part of my life. However, now that my mom and dad have passed, it is just us.

Growing up, my family and I were very close-knit. My parents had always been supportive of our career choices and even the decisions we took.

My grandmother referred the job that I did for the state of California to me; we were always taught to put our careers first. The support from my family from an early age helped kick-start my career and the purchasing of my first house.

As a teenager, I always wanted to start working at an early age. This was largely influenced by the way my mother and my grandmother were career-oriented and that stuck with me. I got my first job at sixteen, and like all other sixteen-year-olds, it was at McDonald's. While many people find this stressful, I stuck around for four years and got to a good position before I quit.

Starting early with my career helped me a lot because I wanted to be independent and wanted to be able to afford my own expenses. Eventually, after quitting my job from McDonald's, I went to a check-cashing place where I was able to get my first apartment. I was twenty-one, but I had to get it cleared with my parents first because we have always been a close family.

I often find myself feeling extremely grateful for being able to go from one loving family to another. George and I worked on building our careers individually and together.

Thinking back to my teenage years, I always wanted to go into hotel management. Needless to say, this did not go as planned. My career took a different route than what I had planned, but it got me where I am today. However, one thing that I had always hoped for was that I would get to travel. I remember sitting in my room as a teenager thinking about all the places in the world that I could go to, which makes me wonder how funny life can be.

When people asked me about why I was never married before George, I do not really know what to say. It clicked when I met him; it was like I had been going all my life not really looking for something but now he was here, and this was good.

I was always a very late bloomer when it came to dating and men. Before George, I only dated two or three men, but it was never anything very serious. I had a set list of boundaries that I kept at par that might have made some people stay away from me and my life; this included the discussion of where I lived with people I was dating. Even my first actual relationship was at twenty-one, when someone asked me out at McDonald's, and stayed persistent. All my life it was me, God, family, my career, and my goals. Whoever I met along the way, I kept my wall up until I met George.

Even with George, I kept my privacy for a month. I did not want him to like me for anything other than me, which is why taking him straight to my house felt like a difficult task for me.

Many times, I think back to why I had not been into the dating scene as any teenager or twenty-year-old would be, and it is mostly because of the way my social gathering was never revolving around that. Dating was not a prerequisite to be around the people I loved, and neither was finding my one true love.

After we relocated to Arizona, I often thought back to losing my house, letting go of my life that I had there. It made me wonder if things had been different, how that would be. How being with a truck driver meant moving cities, but not losing my independence. It was my life, with some advances and love. However, that never made me despise my decision or regret it for one second. I loved where I was, and I loved whom I was with.

Our first real adventure came while we were dating. For the first time ever, I was going with him to work; me on the highway in the Big Rig for the first time ever.

The road trip was a revelation for me; the truck itself is like a small on-the-go apartment for all the truck drivers. Thinking back to the night we spent in the truck, around 11:00 p.m., George parked the truck near the end of the highway and said, "Time to sleep." I still remember being shocked at what he was saying. My mind still could not process that we could sleep on the highway, but he closed the lights and went to bed. I stayed up the entire night and watched as more trucks started to pull up nearby and dimming their own lights. It felt out of place to me, but the more the trucks pulled up, the more I realized what a different world this was for all of them.

The next morning, when George woke up, I told him I was now going to sleep because he was up, and I felt safer. We then proceeded to go to a truck stop, where they had several bathrooms, a comfortable place to cool off. The whole trip was a revelation for me. There is a completely different world out there for truckers that I never realized. From there, we went back home, but the trip was the most fun I had in a long time.

For George and me, it was never about the money. Losing everything made us realize that even with nothing, we had each other and that was always enough. Even amid all the trauma of leaving behind everything and starting over, we managed to keep our little date traditions going—going on trips and managing to have "us" time.

Something that I had always admired about the way our relationship was the lack of monetary obsession we had, or obligations. Nothing was ever forced, social obligations; events such as anniversaries were never celebrated with grand gifts. The gifts that actually meant something were the ones that were not equivalent to thousands of dollars, but things that were thought of.

Every state he has ever been to I have a postcard from there. That is what I love—a love that makes you wonder, a love that is kind, and a love that does not make you hurt your pockets. To have fun with each other is what always kept us going. Small surprises like showing up early, getting flowers, or even something as silly as a large tiger plushy.

At the end of the day, the real adventure is just being with him every day, waking up, showing up, and being hopelessly in love with each other regardless of the money, the place, or even the people.

CHAPTER 8

Just You and I

Throughout our lives, George and I had gone through most of it alone. Even when we had not met each other, our lives were surrounded by our work, our career, and our families. I lived alone for most of my adult life; George was always on the road, so we barely had time for separate family life. Do not get me wrong; we were both close to our families. It just was not in our immediate plans to have our own, but when you meet the love of your life, you think about these things. George always wanted kids, though; he was excited for us to start a family together.

When you enter your early thirties, you start to think about having children, maybe a naughty boy that reminds you of your husband or a sweet little angel girl that is your carbon copy. You start to think of these things. So naturally, so did we. We wanted a family together. It was never because we did not know we would be happy just us, but it was because we wanted to create a life. A happy family of maybe us two and two kids.

I got pregnant early on in our marriage and eventually lost our baby. After that, George and I had so much to deal with that we didn't give up. We thought of alternatives and settled on adoption as one that fit us best. We still wanted a family. Even during the hardest of times, with us downsizing on our expenses, moving to different places, George coming off the road, me getting laid off, and even getting a hysterectomy, we still wanted a child. We stayed strong and stood by each other during this chaotic time.

As time went by, this thought of adoption always lingered over our heads. We tried multiple times, baby classes, adoption agencies, and whatnot, but somehow, it still got derailed for one reason or another. Looking back now, it made sense why it kept being postponed; God always had a plan for us and indeed, h e knows best.

Now that both George and I were in our midforties, the adoption seemed like starting all over again. Therefore, we decided that we would not adopt a newborn baby, not because we did not want one, but only because it would be cheating them of the joy of seeing their parents grow old. We would already be old by the time they were in their teens, so we decided we would not adopt a newborn baby. However, we still wanted a baby even if we would not hold them like a newborn child.

Even after being careful about the details, thinking everything through, making it through every mess life had put us in. There always felt like something was lingering over our heads no matter where we were in our lives.

I still remember the day George and I sat down together. The day was so mundane that I do not even remember the date, but we sat down as we always did. We had our monthly family meeting. It was now time to make the decision; we could not put it off any longer.

Thinking back now, it seems so silly that we both did want the same thing even back then but kept the other person's happiness over our own. George asked me what I wanted to do about the adoption. I asked him. Somehow, we landed on the same answer; we both did not want to adopt a child anymore. It felt like it was not meant for us anyway; we talked about it and thought it through before deciding that it was okay.

George asked me, "It is just going to be you and me. You okay with that?" and I was. I was more than okay with that. We realized somewhere along with that conversation that we were what we needed all along. Through all the financial problems, the bankruptcy, losing a child, and dealing with being apart from each other, we were all we needed and wanted.

As soon as we had this conversation, it felt like a weight had been lifted from our shoulders. These past few years had been hard on both of us, and this thought of eventually adopting always lingered at the back of our minds. Getting it out in the open and deciding against it felt oddly liberating to both of us.

We were happy, though; that was never in question. We had kids all around us, especially our nephews and that was enough for us. Once we said it aloud, we were finally able to let it go. It was no longer holding us back. It was just going to be us two, and we were okay with that. We were both continually dealing with so many things, enjoying our life and being silly that even after we took this decision of not having kids, the spark never died.

Thinking about it now, it was God's plan all along; all the hardships we went through had to lead us to the life we live now. For years, I never felt like I was missing something because I had a child named George; I never needed another baby because I had to deal with my current one.

We had a balance now; we found what works for us and made it work for us. Being a truck driver's wife is hard enough as it is, and when I see other truck driver's wives who have children, it makes me wonder. How different life would have been if we had gone for that option. I commend all those wives who have the double-parent role while their partner is away at work. Parenthood is a full-time job, and I applaud those who are holding down the home front. I have much respect for all those parents dealing with so many other things and still give their children everything they need.

Even though I was up for the challenge, I wanted to test the waters, and I would have done it for George, for me, and our little family. We are happier now though, more than we could have ever been if we had taken that decision because women who do that without their partner actively present every day are superheroes.

George and I were never conventional anyway; we did not need to keep up with society. There was never any pressure from either side to conform to the rules of a civilized society. We did not need a nuclear family to be happy, nor did we ever think that. We made very different choices than the people around us, and every day, I am glad that we did.

Now that everything had been decided, it was just going to be us. Things felt lighter somehow. We continued to plan our date nights and our trips together. Even when we moved to a smaller house, we realized we never needed that space.

We always dreamt of doing many things together, set milestones, but none of them mattered at the end of the day. If life taught us anything, it was that George and I were going to be okay, whether it was on the road or in a one-bedroom apartment or a twelve-bedroom house.

Losing a child was difficult on us; sacrificing all that, losing my job, George shifting between companies, going on the road, and filing for bankruptcy—it was all tough. We made it though. Through it all, we stuck around, and we made it.

Now, it was just George and me, and neither one of us could be happier.

CHAPTER 9

Happy Ever After

"Happy ever after," something we have all heard of. Growing up, it was in every movie, every book, and even in every cartoon. The princess meets the prince, and they live in a far-off wonderful land and live happily ever after. However, even after I was fed all those things from a very early age, I never believed myself to be one of those people who would look forward to it.

Even when I met George, I did not immediately fall in love as I have mentioned before. Looking back now, I only agreed to a free meal, not knowing what I would be getting myself into. George, however, claims he was head over heels the moment he saw me. Cannot blame him, right!

George and I have never conformed to the rules of society; we never went through the meeting and talking twenty-four hours a day, seven days a week, because it was never practical for us. Neither of us thought we had missed out; we never got to go out every day, even initially.

Nevertheless, we made it. It sounds surreal to even say it aloud; we made it. As we near fifteen beautiful years of marriage, the words "I did not marry you for your eggs" echoes in my brain from time to time. I often think back to the devastating news of us having to lose our child, and me having to have a hysterectomy all in two days, and how scared I felt on that night at the hospital. I think back to it and wonder if George had said yes to leaving me when I gave him the option, how different would our lives have been. Every time my mind wanders off to what could have been, I look over to my side and find George just as majestic as the first time I saw him.

"He's here," I tell myself in the middle of the night, as if to reassure myself.

Even amid the worst of the worst days, intense arguments, and the pain of being apart, George and I never stopped showing up. That was the agreement, and we both pulled through. Sometimes, it shocks me. We are here, we have made it this far, and it is only just the beginning of us growing old together.

Many people around us always ask us how we did it. How fifteen years of marriage felt like a second because we were so in love, and how even after all this time, we looked at each other with the same amount of love. I think about it, and the answer is always love. The reason each individual love another, the reason every person in the world has been made for another, and the reasons there is still hope.

We have had the craziest of adventures I still remember. Back in the days, when I knew when George was coming home, I knew he would use the back entrance to come in, so I hung my lingerie on the back door for him to find the minute he gets home. We still do these things, and it keeps the spark alive. Every time George finds a piece of lingerie or I come home to him, surprising me back from the road, it still feels like the first time.

People always talk about the concept of love fading, and I used to wonder if that was true. After years of silently pondering, I realized it is not the love that fades, it is the effort that fades. When people look at George and me going on trips and doing our weekly or monthly dates, they only see the good side of it. They do not see the sacrifices that we have to make to get there, to be able to afford that cruise or that fancy dinner every month.

People like to pinpoint that we have our spark alive because we can afford to do this, but they do not realize the reality of the situation. Being a truck driver comes with a tremendous amount of uncertainty; you never know when you might have to shift companies, and when that happens, you need to bring out your savings to stay afloat. However, even when we feel like we might not do something for each other, we plan. We plan dates, cruises, and mini trips a year in advance to be able to pay off without drowning in debts. That to me is the reason we made it. The reason the love never faded is that we did not let it fade.

Year after year, month after month, George and I go through a million things, and yet we come out the other side stronger and more in love than we were before. The meaning of marriage to me was always showing up, and that is what we do.

George and I structured our lives in a different way from everyone around us; we never took the traditional route to anything. Even now, after years of being married, we prefer enjoying each other's company as opposed to going out to a party.

The past few years have been incredibly hard; we have been through so much. Being in our midthirties made us realize the reality of our situation; when we were downsizing because of the bankruptcy, I remember George and I felt disheartened because it felt like we were going in reverse. However, with every hardship we have faced, we realized at the end of the day, us being together is all that matters.

Something that I recommend to all the couples out there has to be managing their finances to be able to afford a getaway with their significant others. Every year, George and I have our little vacation jar to fill over the year with loose change. Not only does this give us extra disposal cash for when we do get to go out, but it also gives us a good idea about our spending.

At the end of the day, George and I always circle back to our cozy room and snuggle together without worrying about where we are and how we are. When we lost our house, downsized to an apartment, and lost everything, we realized that we did not need the big place or the extra rooms—all we needed was each other.

Going through all that we went through, one thing I have realized is that being a trucker's wife is not easy at all. However, I would advise every wife out there is never to plan something by dates. A truck driver's life is very different from any other job; they are on the road, and things can always change when you are on the road. So it is always best not to plan anything ahead of time.

If you are a trucker's wife reading this, please remember that it is so much better to take life one day at a time, be as flexible as possible, and let things unroll in front of you. There have been times when George has told me he is coming home, but something comes up, and he is not able to show up, which is why we never plan things by dates anymore. One major part of this journey has been the lessons it has taught me. The most important one being: do not expect your spouse home until you see them on the door. This is not an exaggeration; this is how it is, which is what makes it even better and exciting. You have to expect the unexpected so you do not get disappointed when they miss an event, because at the end of the day, it is them that matter, not the date.

If you wonder how George and I keep the spark alive without going by dates, we do our monthly dates and yearly trips, but we just do not mark them by dates because you never know what the work situation will be for him during that time.

George and I have never been the conventional couple, which meant going days without ever thinking about "special events." Every day is a special event. Every time he comes home, we make it a special event, and that is what matters.

George and I came up with a communication way to be able to deal with the anxiety of being away from each other; we agreed on sending each other a text message every two hours and letting the other person know if there was an expected delay in the communication. This meant blizzards or going through a tunnel or if I were going to be busy, we would let the other person know that we would not be available for the next few hours to avoid any unknown anxieties. Even though our system was well thought out, we hit a major bump in this communication cycle. On a Sunday morning, I was on my way to church, and George was on the road. I messaged him that I would not be available during that time and went in the church. When I came out of the church, there was a voicemail on my phone that had been left by the nurse, informing me of George's accident and that he was okay; the floor slipped from underneath my feet in that moment. I had no idea what to do. I started pacing around; there was no contact number, and I could not get a hold of George until the next morning. That had to be the worst night of my life; not knowing where your spouse is, especially under these conditions, is horrifying on so many levels. That is when the reality set in within me. Anything could happen; a tire could blow up; an accident could happen. The call that he made the next morning and said, "Babe, I am okay" was the most calming thing I have ever heard; my entire life came back to focus.

This is what being a truck driver's wife means, and while many of the wives out there might feel like they are alone in feeling all the things we feel, always remember, you are never alone. My advice to all the truck driver's wives, especially the ones with kids, is always to keep the spark alive; if your husband is coming back home, get a sitter for the night and have fun with your spouse.

This was our story; I hope it resonates with the women who might find it difficult to describe everything they feel. It has been a rollercoaster, one I would go on repeatedly as long as he was with me.

And so George and I lived happily ever after.

ABOUT THE AUTHOR

Home town Fresno, Ca High School Graduate Centennial High School Compton Ca. And Some College. I love hosting parties, and gathering with family, friends and loves travelling

Wife of a OTR Driver comes with a lot hate, which kepts me busy.

Right now, Im currently working from home trying to adjust to new normal. George has gotten his brokers license and in the process of buying another truck. I'll keep you posted.

CPSIA information can be obtained
at www.ICGtesting.com
Printed in the USA
LVHW031538150721
692621LV00001B/85